WILD
ANIMALS

Anna Sproule

TREASURE
PRESS

CONTENTS

The wide, spreading ears of this African elephant
are one of the main features that mark it out
from its Indian relative.

INTRODUCTION

An animal is any living organism that is not plant or plant-like. This may sound obvious but although a tree is readily recognized as a plant and a cow as an animal, when we come to the microscopic forms of life a distinction is not so easily made. The best thing to say is that a plant can manufacture its own food; an animal cannot. This still leaves organisms such as bacteria and fungi, which cannot manufacture food, and one day we shall relegate these to a third kingdom.

The earliest plants began some two thousand million years ago and it was not until about seven hundred million years ago that plants, in the form with which we are familiar, and animals put in an appearance. At first there were only backbone-less animals, the Invertebrata, and they all lived in water; that is, in the sea. Then, about 500 million years ago, appeared the first animals that possessed the beginnings of a backbone. They were the forerunners of the Vertebrata or animals with backbones, from which sprang the earliest fishes. It was another hundred million years before any life appeared on land. Plants were the first to invade the land, followed by some of the invertebrates. Conspicuous among these were those invertebrates that gave rise to insects. Once the land vegetation had become established and the insects, life on land became possible for some of the larger animals. For this to happen meant a drastic change in the animals themselves and in their way of life.

There are some fishes today that breathe air, using lungs, and also take up oxygen from water through their gills. One of these is the lungfish. The mudskippers, fishes living in tropical estuaries, habitually come out on land and move about using their paired fins as crutches. We can surmise from these that some early fishes did something very like the mudskippers, and at the same time had lungs like the modern lungfish.

Animals that live partly on land and partly in water are said to be amphibious. From the first amphibious fishes evolved animals which were wholly air-breathing as adults and, in addition, had developed legs in place of paired fins. The earliest of these, of which we have knowledge, was like a huge newt, six feet long. From it, through numerous fossil remains, can be traced the evolution of the present-day Amphibia, the newts and salamanders, frogs and toads. All these, even today, are not wholly independent of water, including those that spend the greater part of their lives out of it. They must go back to water to breed. Their offspring are fish-like tadpoles which breathe at first through gills and later through lungs. The adults themselves, although equipped with lungs and having legs for locomotion, must keep moist for the simple reason that they do most of their breathing through their skin; this must be kept damp if respiration is to continue.

Newts and salamanders are shaped very much like lizards and other four-legged reptiles, and there is every reason to believe that reptiles evolved from amphibians. For this to happen two fundamental changes had to occur. There had to be a change in the skin so that it no longer dried up out of water. This was largely met by the development of a coating of scales, but there had to be other changes in the skin itself. After all, fishes are covered with scales. The other major change was that the females laid eggs enclosed in parchment-like shells and containing fluid in which the tadpoles could live without drying up.

The first amphibians appeared 360 million years ago and about sixty million years later came the first reptiles. Then a remarkable thing happened. These newcomers, the reptiles, began to diversify. This always has happened, in the course of geological time, when a new type of animal arises. The reptiles budded off, so to speak, numerous species which today we know as the tuatara, the

A European red deer in its native woodland; the fine antlers show that it is a full-grown stag.

crocodiles, tortoises and turtles and eventually the dinosaurs. In due course, also, some reptiles returned to the sea to become the ichthyosaurs and plesiosaurs, and others took to the air – the flying reptiles, known as the pterodactyls. Some of the dinosaurs grew to tremendous sizes, like Diplodocus and Stegosaurus, and, all in all, the reptiles flourished exceedingly and for two hundred million years dominated the world. This period of domination is known as The Age of Reptiles. There were plenty of other animals around but they were eclipsed by the numbers and sizes attained by the reptiles. Then, apparently quite suddenly in terms of geological history, the dinosaurs became extinct and it is still a mystery why this should have happened.

Before this sudden extinction had occurred, however, two important events took place. The mammals came into being and so did the birds, both differing strikingly from any animals that had preceded them, especially in one respect. They were warmblooded, whereas all animals before them had been cold-blooded.

These two terms require explanation because, as they stand, they can be misleading. When we say an animal is coldblooded we mean that the temperature of its body is about the same as that of its surroundings. If the day is cold the animal's body is cold; when the surrounding air warms up so the animal's body temperature rises. The body temperature of some so-called coldblooded animals may rise above that of its surroundings due to the animal's own exertions. This happens, for example, in some fast-swimming fishes, such as the tunny, or tuna. To avoid misunderstanding therefore, the scientist uses the word poikilothermic instead of coldblooded.

Birds and mammals are so built that they control the temperature of their bodies so that it remains approximately the same no matter what the temperature of the surrounding air (or water, in the case of aquatic animals such as whales). We speak of them therefore as homoiothermic. This is a more precise term because it means keeping the temperature at the same level all the time instead of having it fluctuate with changes in the surroundings. Mammals, for example, can control their temperature most obviously by sweating when the surroundings are too warm and shivering when the external temperature drops.

We now know that some of the dinosaurs were at least partially homoiothermic and it is almost certain that, from these dinosaurs, birds, on the one hand, and reptiles, on the other, are

descended. It is easier to believe in birds being descended from reptiles than it is to believe mammals had this same origin. The scaly legs of birds resemble closely the legs of reptiles. The earliest known fossil bird, the archaeopteryx, looks very much like a reptile that has grown feathers instead of scales except on the lower parts of the legs and on the feet.

To believe in mammals having reptilian ancestors is less easy but fortunately there are two kinds of animals in Australia that bridge the gap. Both are truly mammals in that they suckle their newborn young. They are the platypus or duckbill and the echidna or spiny anteater; together they are known as the egg-laying mammals. Both have a hairy coat although in echidna much of the coat is transformed into spines. From that point of view also they are mammals. Nevertheless, and this is the interesting point, in much of their anatomy, in some parts of their skeleton, for example, they show decided reptilian features.

Another group of mammals living today in Australia is the pouch-bearers, or marsupials, including kangaroos, koalas and many others. These are nearer to the true mammals, especially in bearing live young, yet they still retain a few reptilian features.

What has been said does not mean that both birds and mammals are descended from the same semi-homoiothermic dinosaurs. Each probably sprang from a different group within the dinosaurs as a whole.

One advantage of the homoiothermic condition is that an animal can remain active even when the temperature drops or rises, provided such changes are not extreme. So birds and mammals are assured of longer periods of activity each day and for more days a year, despite the changing seasons, and in a wider range of latitudes.

In mammals at least, there is a marked increase in the organization of the brain, bringing with it a higher intelligence. So it comes about that the mammals, which first appeared just over two hundred million years ago, now dominate the world as surely as the reptiles did during the Age of Reptiles. Among the mammals, and dominating them, is the human species – the most intelligent, adaptable and destructive of them all.

The rhinoceros (*opposite, top*) and the hornbill (*opposite, below*) appear to have something in common. The bird's 'horn' is less heavy than it looks. The rhino's horn is really matted hair.

AMPHIBIANS AND REPTILES

Frogs are amphibians: born in the water, they breathe air and live on land when adult (*below*). Some even live in trees (*opposite*). Some of the tree-frog species seldom come down to ground-level, but most frogs live near or in (*left*) fresh water or in damp places. It is here that they lay their eggs and that the tadpoles develop.

Snakes, like all reptiles, are descended from amphibians. The world's first reptiles appeared about 300 million years ago; the snakes themselves, comparative late-comers, arrived on the scene 150 million years later.

None have legs – but some snakes such as pythons and boa constrictors still retain traces of a pelvis and hind legs within their bodies. For this reason, it is believed that snakes are lizards that have lost their limbs. (The slowworm is a limbless lizard.)

There are about 2700 different species of snake in existence today. The only countries in the world that have no native snakes are New Zealand and Ireland. Snakes are most numerous in the tropics and in warm climates, since their body temperature depends on that of their surroundings, and they become sluggish in cold conditions. All are adapted to eating large, infrequent meals.

Snakes differ in their methods of catching their prey. Both the Papuan tree-python (*below*) and the king python (*opposite*) are constrictors. They squeeze their victims to death in the massive

coils of their bodies. The enormous anaconda –
which, with a maximum length of over 9m (30ft),
is the biggest snake in the world – does the same.
But vipers like the one shown overleaf subdue
their prey by poisoning it.

A snake's venom is secreted from glands
connected to its teeth. When it bites its victim,
the teeth act like a hypodermic syringe. The
victim is either weakened by the injected
poison, or paralyzed outright. Poisonous snakes
include the cobras, rattlesnakes, mambas and
vipers; the adder is a viper species.

Like all marine members of its family, the sea-going turtle (*below*) has a flattened, streamlined appearance. Full-grown specimens can reach a length of three feet or more. The flipper-like legs cannot be drawn into the shell and are an important aid to fast swimming. On land, though, the turtle is slow and clumsy. Terrestrial turtles, or tortoises, are also slow movers. Their chief defence lies in the layers of horny scales and bone that make up their shells. Although turtles and tortoises breath air, some can stay underwater for hours.

The water lizard (*below*) is a member of the biggest group of reptiles in the world: the saurians. All saurians – currently some 3000 species – are lizards of one sort or another. Some, like the water lizards and the marine iguanas, are aquatic; many are good climbers and a few can take to the air, gliding from tree to tree with the help of flaps of skin along the sides of the body. In size they range from the geckos (which measure less than 77mm (3ins) long) to the monitors, one of which – the Komodo dragon – may reach 3m (10ft).

Overleaf: a group of crocodiles take their ease in the warm waters of a tropical river. The largest members of the order Crocodylia, they can grow to a length of over 6m (20ft). Their cousins, the alligators, are slightly smaller and have narrower heads; another difference between them is that the fourth tooth in the crocodile's lower teeth remains visible when the jaw is shut. Both crocodiles and alligators are carnivorous. They kill their prey by dragging it underwater and drowning it. Crocodiles, in particular, have an ill-deserved reputation as man-eaters.

BIRDS

The distant ancestors of both the kingfisher (*below*) and the
nightingale (*opposite*) were a group of flying reptiles that,
over 150 million years ago, sprouted feathers instead of
scales. The flying reptiles themselves died out – but the
total number of their feathered descendants now stands at
about 8650 species, ranging from the huge (and non-flying)
ostriches to the tiny hummingbirds. In spite of the
differences between them, all birds have much in common.
They all lay eggs. They all have good sight. And – like
mammals but unlike reptiles – they maintain their bodies at
a constant temperature.

Owls

Most birds eat and hunt by day and sleep by night. Owls, however, work the other way round. They are the best-known of all nocturnal birds, and many of their most striking characteristics are linked to this preference for night-time activity.

The challenging stare of the owl on the opposite page owes much of its intensity to the fact that owls have binocular, or 'two-eyed', vision. As explained on page 63, this highly efficient sight mechanism is shared by many other nocturnal animals. Although owls cannot swivel their eyes in their sockets, they can turn their heads through a very wide arc instead; if an owl wants to look at something at its side, it can do so with a minimum of noise and movement.

Quietness is also a hallmark of the owl's hunting technique. As shown on the left (*bottom picture*), an owl's plumage is extremely soft and fluffy, and this feature contributes to the bird's almost silent flight. Until the last second, it is not only invisible to its prey – thanks to the darkness – but inaudible as well.

In addition to their keen sight, owls have exceptionally good hearing, and find no difficulty in hunting by ear. Not all owls, however, have such obvious ear-tufts as the long-eared owl (*left, top*), or the Eurasian eagle owl (*left, centre*). The eagle owl, which can grow to 0.7m (2ft 4in), is one of the world's biggest owls, and also one of the fiercest.

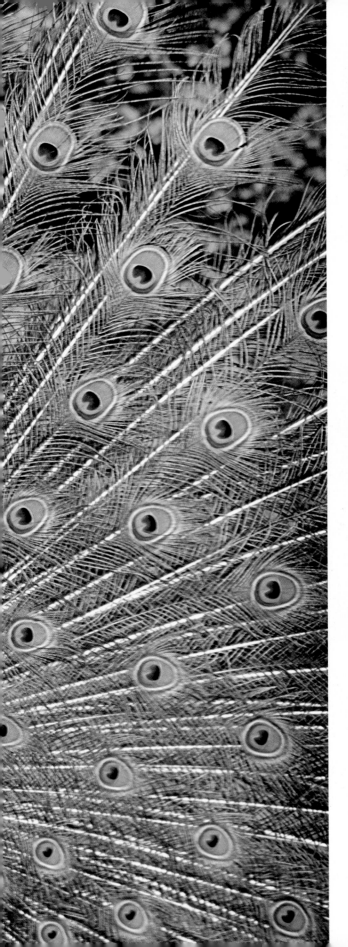

Exotic birds

The scarlet macaws (*above, top*) of South America are among the most brightly coloured birds in the world. The related cockatoo (*above*), with its white plumage and sulphur-yellow crest, is almost as spectacular. But neither can compare for sheer splendour with a common peacock (*left*) in full display. Peafowl belong to the same order of birds as the turkey, the pheasant, and the common farmyard chicken.

Long-legged birds

Although the stork (*opposite*) and the crane (*left, below*) belong to different orders of birds, they both have the long legs and necks that are typical of many species that frequent marshes and rivers, and that live by catching food in water or on marshy ground.

The greater flamingo (*left, top*) has an even longer neck than its stork relatives, and stands on the same stilt-like legs. But its beak is unlike that of any stork; indeed, no other bird in the world has anything like it.

Flamingos feed on small animals and plants they dredge up from the water and mud; since a flamingo's head points directly downwards during feeding, it is the curved upper jaw that does most of the work. The lower one is less movable. Both the beak and the bird's rough-edged tongue help the flamingo sieve its food from the mud.

Greater flamingos are found wild in southern Europe and in Africa, Asia and America, where they live round the Caribbean coast. Another species, the Chilean flamingo, breeds almost down to the southern tip of the American continent. Not all flamingos are as pale as the one shown here; many are a bright pink. But even brightly-coloured birds may 'bleach' when they are kept in zoos.

The ultimate in specialized feeding techniques:
with wings beating at 75 strokes a second, a
hummingbird (*right*) hovers by a flower to drink
its nectar. The bird's tongue, which is shaped
like a tube at the tip, is being used in much the
same way as a drinking-straw.

Not all birds have adapted themselves so
spectacularly to their feeding requirements, but
every bird shows some indication of the links
between itself and its preferred diet. At its
simplest, this is seen in seed-eaters like the
finches. A typical finch beak – whether it
belongs to the zebra finch of Australia or the
hawfinch of Europe and Asia – is massively
built, given the size of its owner. Strong and
conical, it is constructed for dealing with
hard-shelled seeds and fruit stones.

In contrast, birds like swallows – which live on
insects caught on the wing – have small,
somewhat fragile-looking beaks. The important
feature of a swallow's beak is its extra-wide
gape: without this, the bird could not catch
enough insects to survive.

Among the birds of prey, the cruelly-curved
beak is an important aid to tearing up food. But
it is not the birds' main weapon. Most raptors
live by pursuing live prey – usually either bird
or mammal – and seizing it with their
immensely strong feet. (Falconers always wear a
thick glove on the hand that carries the bird to
protect it from the talons.) Owls employ the
same grab-and-hold technique.

Strong legs and feet are also a key characteristic
of the Galliformes or fowl-like birds: the large
order of birds that includes pheasants, grouse,
turkeys, peafowl, and domestic poultry. Many
of these are not good flyers; they run away from
danger. And they make much of their living by
scratching for food on the ground.

ANIMALS UNDER THREAT

The animals described here are just a few of the thousand or so species whose survival is currently under threat. Some members of this group live in the tropics, some in the world's coldest regions. Some are huge, some are tiny. Some swim, some move at ground or tree level, and many fly.

Where survival is concerned all of them are at risk to a lesser or greater degree, and some may already be past the point of no return. In every case, the source of the threat is man. Many species have been hunted for their meat, plumage, fur, by-products or because of their value to collectors. Others have had their natural habitats destroyed by the spread of industry and agriculture. All over the world, countries are now protecting their threatened species by setting up conservation areas and introducing anti-hunting laws. But, in spite of this, the threat continues.

GIANT PANDA *Ailuropoda melanoleuca*
Symbol of the World Wildlife Fund, and one of the world's most famous animals, the Giant Panda, shown on page 46, continues to puzzle scientists. Is it a sort of bear or is it the largest of the raccoons? How long does it live in the wild? How often does it breed? How many are there? Now under strict protection, the Giant Panda owes much of its mystery to two things: it is both rare and extremely shy. It is only found in a single mountainous region of China, thickly forested with bamboo.

A full-grown Giant Panda measures about six feet long. Its black-and-white coat gives it both protection against winter snows and natural camouflage.

Although it eats some meat and fish, the bulk of its diet consists of bamboo shoots; to hold them, it makes use of an extra thumb-like pad on each forepaw.

Giant Pandas are solitary animals, except during the mating season; as far as is known, females only bear a single cub. They have seldom bred in captivity.

BLUE WHALE *Balaenoptera musculus*
The largest animal that has ever lived, the Blue Whale starts life as a four-ton calf, and reaches its full weight of 120 tons or more when it is about 12 years old. By this time, it may measure up to one hundred feet long.

Although Blue Whales have been found all over the world, most of them live in the Antarctic Ocean. From here, they migrate north to warmer water every year for breeding. Females are capable of bearing a calf every other year.

The Blue Whale's diet consists almost entirely of Krill, a kind of shrimp found in the plankton of which it eats several tons a day.

Unlike their relatives, the dolphins and porpoises, Blue Whales are not gregarious. They sometimes form groups, but these are always small. Whether alone or in company, members of this species are shy, and can reach a speed of up to 14 knots to get away from danger.

CALIFORNIA CONDOR *Gymnogyps californianus*
Fossil remains of the huge California Condor have been found in Mexico and in no less than six states of the USA. Its range has now shrunk to California itself, and its numbers can be counted in tens rather than hundreds.

The California Condor is the biggest airborne bird in the world. (The biggest of all are the non-flying ostriches.) The condor measures over 11 feet from wing tip to wing tip.

Both head and neck are bare; the plumage is black, with white markings on the wings. A dark ruff of feathers circles the throat.

Condors are members of the vulture family and, as such, are carrion-eaters. Dead cattle form an important part of the California Condor's diet. Anything but prolific breeders, females lay only one egg every other year.

BLACK RHINOCEROS *Diceros bicornis*
The Black Rhinoceros of Africa, like the White Rhinoceros, can be distinguished from most

Asiatic members of its family by having two horns. Its preferred habitat is dry scrubland and, unlike the White Rhino, it is a browser rather than a grazer. It has a long, pointed upper lip that it uses for picking leafy shoots and twigs. As a consequence, it is also called the hook-lipped rhinoceros, whereas the White Rhino's alternative name is square-lipped. The Black Rhino is famed for its aggressive temperament, and is liable to launch its two-ton bulk into a charge against any intruder. A major cause of the decline of rhino numbers is the belief held in some parts of the world that powdered rhino horn is a potent aphrodisiac.

PRZEWALSKI'S HORSE *Equus przewalskii przewalskii*

Possibly extinct in the wild – no one knows. But it is beginning to seem likely that the world's only Przewalskis are those in zoos or reserves. The species gets its name from the Russian explorer Colonel N. M. Przewalski, who, in 1881, discovered a herd of wild, pony-like horses living on the edge of the Gobi Desert. A relative of all the domestic horses of Mongolia and China, the Przewalski is the last wild horse species left. It stands 14 hands high and is solidly built, with a large head, short neck and back, and strong legs. Its up-standing, crest-like mane lacks a forelock.

The coat varies according to the season: a Przewalski in summer is pale yellow and relatively short-haired, but its shaggy winter coat is darker. Mane and tail are both dark. A distinctive feature is the black 'eel stripe' that the Przewalski carries down the length of its back during the summer months. It also has a fainter stripe across the shoulders and dark-coloured bars on its legs: marks that are a reminder of its close family connections with both the donkeys and the zebras.

The main reasons for the species' ruinous decline over the years include hunting (now illegal) and the take-over of its grazing grounds by nomadic shepherds.

ORANG-UTAN *Pongo pygmaeus*

Second biggest of the great apes, the Orang-utan is the only one living outside Africa. Its home is the lowland jungle of Borneo and Sumatra, and its threatened status stems partly from the fact that large tracts of this jungle territory have been taken over for timber production and are being seriously reduced in size.

Orang-utans, unlike gorillas and chimpanzees, seldom frequent the forest floor. Their feeble legs – combined with enormously powerful arms – restrict them to a tree-dwelling life. Even in the trees, however, their movements are much less agile than those of the related, but much smaller, Gibbon.

The average weight of an Orang-utan is in the region of 200lb. Although they eat some animal matter, their main food is fruit: principally that of the durian. Like the other great apes, they usually live and forage in family groups.

SIBERIAN TIGER *Panthera tigris altaica*

Experts believe that the original homeland of all tigers – whether they eventually settled in India, Sumatra, Iran, or elsewhere – was northern Asia. In this thickly-furred race, Siberia still has its own native tiger; but, like all other races of tiger, it has been hunted to the point where its survival is now at risk.

Tigers tend to become bigger and paler the farther north they live. The Siberian is the biggest of all: some have been recorded as measuring 13 feet or more in length. (The average length for a tiger elsewhere is about nine feet.)

The stripes that the whole family carry are an indication of its preferred habitat. Whether they live in the cool uplands of Korea or the tropical islands of the East Indies, tigers shun open spaces and stick to woods and other areas of dense cover. (The Siberian itself tends to frequent thick reedbeds.)

Tigers cannot tolerate great heat, and seek thick shade – or water – in order to keep themselves cool. They are good swimmers.

MAMMALS

All mammals have one thing in common: their young are fed on milk produced by their mothers. That apart, however, the differences between them can be enormous. Some mammals give birth on dry land, others in the water. Some walk or run; others jump, swim, fly or swing through trees. They sleep in holes, nests, floating rafts of seaweed, or underground burrows. And their range of diet is vast. The lion is possibly the world's most famous mammal. But the following pages show some other contenders for the title.

The big cats

Largest of all the cats, lions are in some ways similar to the domestic tabby. Both are meat-eaters, or carnivores; both can cope with big meals at long intervals; both alternate spells of activity with periods of total relaxation. The lioness opposite demonstrates a typical resting position.

However, lions differ from other cats – both large and small – in two main ways. The first is the more immediately striking of the two: it consists of the dense, shaggy mane that distinguishes the males of the species (*below*). The other difference is that lions are social animals. They live and hunt in family groups, or prides. The leader of the pride is always a male; the rest of the group is made up of lionesses and their cubs and young not fully grown. When the males are old enough to challenge the leadership of the pride they are driven away.

Even though they look alike, the cheetah (*below*) and the leopard (*opposite*) belong to completely different genera. The leopard is a close relative of the lion, the tiger and other big cats such as the jaguar. The cheetah differs from all other cats in running down its prey instead of stalking it, and in having claws that are only partially retractile.

Leopards can be found in Africa, Arabia, India, southern Asia and as far north as Korea. They tend to keep to thick cover, where their spotted coats blend with the sun-dappled undergrowth.

Expert climbers, they can haul an antelope carcass high into a tree with ease, to consume it at leisure.

Cheetahs have a more restricted range. They were once common in India, where they were used for hunting. Today, they are found mainly in Africa and in parts of the Middle East. But even here they have become very rare.

Their long legs and extremely supple backs make cheetahs the fastest land animals in the world. Over short bursts of about a quarter mile, they can reach speeds of up to 70mph. An

additional aid to speed is their claws, which –
unlike those of other cats – can only be partially
drawn back into the paws. They help a
sprinting cheetah grip the ground firmly.

Previous page: a Bengal tiger cools off. Tigers
cannot tolerate the fierce heat of the tropical sun
and always lie up in thick shade or in water
during the hottest part of the day. In addition
to the Bengal tiger there are six other races: the
Siberian, Chinese, Caspian, Sumatran, Javan
and Bali tigers.

Social animals

Some animals, such as cats and bears, lead solitary lives. The zebras (*below*) and the giraffes (*opposite*) both live in groups, and would be highly disturbed if cut off from their fellows for any length of time. They are, in fact, social animals.

Zebras – like their close relatives, the horses – are herd-dwellers. So are most species of antelope and deer but the social urge is not confined to hoofed animals. It is also extremely strong in (among others) monkeys, wild dogs, elephants (*overleaf*), seals, dolphins, rabbits, many rodents, birds – and man.

Elephants

Right: herds of African elephants wander peacefully through Kenya's Amboseli Game Reserve. Mount Kilimanjaro towers in the background. Biggest of all living land animals, both the African elephant and its slightly smaller Indian cousin are really Ice Age animals that have survived to the present day. (Great size and weight were typical characteristics of the Ice Age fauna; elephants of that period that did not survive include the mammoths and woolly elephants of Siberia and North America.)

A full-grown African bull elephant may weigh six tons and stand 3m (10ft) high or more; his opposite number in India is two tons less in weight. In addition, the Indian elephant can be distinguished easily from the African by its smaller ears. Both species have tusks which are really incisor teeth that have grown forwards and outwards. These are markedly longer in the African elephant but in the Indian female elephant they are usually not visible.

An elephant eats a variety of vegetable matter, from fruit to sapling trees, and its tusks help it dig up trees and plants. It can push over even large trees with its forehead and with its trunk it can tear off branches, gather fruit and leaves. An elephant also drinks with its trunk. A thirsty elephant siphons up water with its trunk, and then squirts it into its mouth. It uses the same squirting technique for washing and for dust-bathing.

The results of another washing method are demonstrated on the right: the elephant has emerged from a pool in which only the top of its head has been above water. Under such circumstances, the trunk is held high and used as a breathing aid. The domesticated elephants used in Asia for haulage and pack-transport all belong to the Indian species; African elephants of the type shown here have never been domesticated. The war elephants which were used by the Romans and Carthaginians are believed, in fact, to have come from Africa. The theory is that they belonged to a now-extinct species (or race) that lived in the north of the continent and were brought into use by the ancient Egyptians.

Primates

The gorilla (*opposite*) and the baboons (*left* and *below*) are primates: they are both members of the most advanced order of mammals. The highly social baboons, who live in large troops and are notorious crop-raiders, are the less advanced mentally of the two; in contrast, the brains of the gorilla and of the other great apes are second only to man's in development.
In spite of their impressive bulk, gorillas are peaceable unless provoked. They live and forage for food (fruit and leaves) in family parties, led by a senior 'silverback' or full-grown male. The groups spend much of the day on the ground, but usually retire to the trees at night. They build new nests each evening.

Mammals in the sea

The dolphin (*below*) and the Alaskan fur seals (*opposite*) have two things in common; both are mammals that have adapted themselves to a marine life, and both are highly social animals. Dolphins – which are extremely intelligent – travel and play in large schools, while the fur seals display the social urge at its most organized level. Breeding colonies like the one opposite are governed by complex territorial rules set by the vast males or 'beachmasters'. Each male lays claim to a harem of females, who first give birth to the pups they are carrying, and mate with their bull shortly afterwards. Other males intruding on a beachmaster's territory are chased off.

The fur seals can still make adequate use of their limbs on land but dolphins and whales have lost all trace of hind limbs and their front ones resemble fins.

Bears and pandas

The large bears of the northern hemisphere – the brown bear (*right*), the Kodiak (*top left*) and the Polar (*bottom left*) – are among the most formidable wild animals in the world. Although their popular image is one of amiable chubbiness, they are, in fact, extremely strong and – in spite of their lumbering, flat-footed gait – very fast. Their powerful claws, their teeth, and their sheer weight make them all the more dangerous.

Of the three types of bear shown here, the Kodiak fishing for salmon in an Alaskan river is the largest. With an average length of about nine feet, it is the biggest of all the brown bears. The Polar bear is only slightly smaller. The European brown bear – to which the Kodiak is so closely related that it may even be a member of the same species – is about 1.8m (6ft) long. The non-arctic bears eat meat, fish, fruit, honey and insects. The Polar, however, is almost totally carnivorous. Its chief prey is seal, although it also eats fish.

Bear-like but not a bear, the giant panda of China (*left, centre*) lives mainly on bamboo shoots. Sometimes, though, it will eat small birds and fish. When fishing, it uses the same paw-flipping technique as the true bears (see also page 28).

Ungulates

The proverb about the difficulty of sorting the sheep from the goats is based all too truly on fact. The group of ibex (*below*) are wild goats. The argali of Central Asia (*opposite, top right*) is a wild sheep. Part of the confusion, which bothers scientists as much as it does the ordinary observer, stems from the fact that both wild goats and wild sheep have hairy coats. Their bones are similar, too. Sheep were first domesticated for their meat rather than their wool, and it was only when man learned to operate selective breeding programmes that woolly sheep came on the scene.

Both sheep and goats are even-toed ungulates: that is, their toes end in hoofs rather than claws, and they have an even number of these hoofed toes on each foot. The impala (*opposite, bottom*) is also an even-toed ungulate, as is the red deer (*opposite, top left*) . Sheep, goats, and impalas all belong to the same family as cattle, the Bovidae.

The impala is one of the world's best long-jumpers, beating even the kangaroo; it can cover 30 feet or more in a single bound. Like many other members of the cattle family, impalas are gregarious by nature, and live in medium-sized or large herds. Red deer, also gregarious, live in single-sex groups most of the year, and join forces only in the autumn.

The spreading structures on the deer's head are not horns but antlers. Horns such as those of the ibex and the impala are permanent growths; the deer's antlers are renewed annually. As is the case with most deer, antlers are only carried by the males.

Marsupials

Marsupials like the wallaby (*below*), the kangaroo (*opposite*) and the koala (*overleaf*) differ from other mammals in one particular way. They are equipped with pouches in which their young can develop. At birth, a kangaroo is no more than an inch long; even though it is so small, however, it is able to make its way almost immediately into its mother's pouch. A young kangaroo is ready to leave the pouch when it is eight months old, but it will continue to suckle for several months more.

Most marsupials are only found in Australia and the neighbouring islands of Tasmania and New Guinea. They include the bandicoot, the marsupial mouse, the marsupial mole, the flying phalanger, the wombat, the ferocious Tasmanian devil, and the marsupial wolf or thylacine. (The thylacine may now be extinct.)

Exceptions to the 'down under' rule are the

opossums, which live in the southern states of America and in Central and South America. Not all the American opossums have true pouches, however.

Overleaf: a young koala will continue to cling to its mother's back long after leaving her pouch. At birth, koalas are even smaller than kangaroos; they measure 19mm (0.25in) in length. Since the female's pouch opens backwards, however, the new-born koala has less distance to go before finding safety.

Wolves and foxes

Below: did the first dogs look like this? Scientists are still not sure whether the domestic dog is descended from the wolf, the pi dog, the jackal, or a totally different species now extinct. But the common wolf shown below resembles a domestic dog in so many ways that the wolf theory still has numerous supporters.

Like all members of the dog family, wolves are carnivorous. They hunt in family groups (not packs) and display strong loyalty to their group-leaders and fellow group-members. They also have one mate for life.

Red foxes like those opposite can be found in suburban gardens as well as in the woods and fields of the open country. In parks, foxes scavenge through litter-baskets, and among houses they raid dustbins; they also prey on vermin such as rats and mice.

The ground squirrel (*above*), the dormouse (*below*) and the European red squirrel (*opposite*) belong to the huge order of rodents or gnawing animals. In all there are nearly 2000 rodent species, distributed right across the world; they range in size from the 1.2m (4ft) long capybara of South America to mice. Although they belong to the same family, the ground and red squirrels have quite different habits. Ground squirrels tend to live in burrows; red squirrels inhabit the trees. The dormouse is also an expert climber, and is considered as a pest by fruit-growers.

Carnivores

The weasel (*above*) is an outstandingly fierce predator for its size; although less than 30cm (1ft) long, it will attack and kill an animal as big as a rabbit. Like the closely-related stoat (which is larger and has a black tip to the tail) weasels will also steal eggs. Both stoats and weasels are regarded as pests, especially by farmers and gamekeepers. The winter coat of the stoat, however, has a value in the fur trade: stoats that live in cold climates turn white, and their white pelts – which retain the black tail tip – are called ermine.

The raccoon of North America also used to be hunted for its fur, which was made into the once-fashionable coonskin coats. In spite of this, raccoons are still numerous in the USA. (*right*) Although they have a foxy look about them, raccoons belong to the same zoological family as the giant panda. They have a reputation for crop-raiding (and also for emptying suburban dustbins) but streams and ponds are their main sources of food. Using their agile front paws, they dredge through the shallows for fish, frogs, and other aquatic creatures.

Life by the stream

Both the beaver (*left*) and the otter (*opposite*) are river animals. The otter's main diet is fish; the beaver is a vegetarian but the 'beaver pond' (made by the dams it builds across rivers) forms one of the animal's main defences against enemies. Further defences are built into the lodge beavers construct in the middle of the pond; the entrances all start underwater. Beavers are rodents while otters belong to the same family as the polecat (*below*) and the weasel (shown on page 58). Thanks partly to Gavin Maxwell's world-famous book, *Ring of Bright Water*, it is easily the most popular of all the Mustelidae, or weasel-like animals. The polecat, however, has an evil reputation.

Nocturnal creatures

Bats (*above*) and hedgehogs (*right*) are nocturnal animals: that is, they sleep by day and forage by night. Many gardeners – even urban ones – have seen a hedgehog in the early stages of its night-time hunt for slugs, snails and other pests. A pair of insectivorous bats, 'hawking' for flying insects in the lee of a belt of trees or a building, is also a common evening sight. Some bats, including the large flying foxes, are fruit- rather than insect-eaters, while the vampire bat of South America lives on fresh blood sucked from live victims.

The insectivorous bats, in particular, have evolved a system of echo-location which enables them to avoid obstacles while flying at night. The echoes are made by ultra-sonic sounds given out by the bat, which are bounced off any solid surface and picked up by the ears.

Above: the badger, one of the bigger members of the weasel family, is so shy of bright light that even a full moon may make it wary of leaving its burrow, or sett. It is believed to have weak eyesight, and hunts mainly by smell.

The African potto (*left*) is a slow-moving, fruit-eating relative of the monkeys. Like many nocturnal animals, it has large round eyes set into the front of the head rather than the side. Other creatures of the night which possess binocular vision include bushbabies, tarsiers, owls and cats. The night vision of cats is particularly famous: they are able to use what light there is twice with the aid of a reflecting layer behind the retina.

INDEX

FRONT COVER PHOTOGRAPH:
MITCH REARDON/TONY STONE
WORLDWIDE
BACK COVER PHOTOGRAPH:
TONY STONE WORLDWIDE

This edition published in 1990 by
Treasure Press, Michelin House, 81
Fulham Road, London SW3 6RB

© 1979 Cathay Books

ISBN 1 85051 491 7

Produced by Mandarin Offset
Printed in Hong Kong